THE
TOTALLY
PIES
COOKBOOK

THE
TOTALLY
PIES
COOKBOOK

By Helene Siegel & Karen Gillingham

Illustrated by Carolyn Vibbert

CELESTIAL ARTS
BERKELEY, CALIFORNIA

The Totally Pies Cookbook is produced
by becker&mayer!, Kirkland, Washington.

www.beckermayer.com

Printed in Singapore.

Cover design and illustration: Bob Greisen
Interior design and typesetting: Susan Hernday
Interior illustrations: Carolyn Vibbert

Library of Congress Cataloging-in-Publication Data
Siegel, Helene.
    The Totally Pies Cookbook / by Helene Siegel & Karen
    Gillingham; illustrated by Karen Vibbert
            p.   cm.
    ISBN 0-89087-884-6
    1. Pies.   I. Gillingham, Karen   II. Title.
TX773.S465 1998
641.8′652--dc21   98-28586
                        CIP

Celestial Arts Publishing
P.O. Box 7123
Berkeley, CA 94707
Look for all 26 *Totally* books at your local store!

FOR ANDREW

CONTENTS

INTRODUCTION

The real meaning of pie came to me in a flash at my younger son's book fair. It was a weeknight event at his elementary school, and in addition to the books for sale, there was a pizza-and-soda dinner available for those parents too frazzled to worry about the nutrition police.

Since I was testing pie recipes at the time, I brought over a less-than-perfect cherry pie. It was delicious, but the filling was too runny and the lattice crust had not quite achieved that state of burnished Martha Stewart-like perfection I originally had in mind. (Let's face it. It wasn't even anchored to the bottom anymore. It had a life of its own.) The pie was a retest, for sure, but rather than toss it, I brought it over to the fair. It was an experiment. Would kids raised on mass-produced chocolate chip cookies, brownies in a box, and souped-up "nutrition" bars even glance at a messy, old-fashioned, fruit-filled pie?

When I sneaked a peek at the sale table later in the evening, I was pleased. The pie had just about sold out. When the last sloppy slice was picked up by a well-tailored professional mom, she said to no one in particular, "Who has the time to bake a pie?"

She had a point. Who does have the time, or technique, anymore to bake a pie? For those of us who did not grow up attached to the apron strings of a baking mother or grandmother, the tradition is more or less lost. With a pervasive fear of crust-making and many people without so much as a rolling pin in the kitchen, where is the occasional baker to begin?

Start anywhere, and be easy on yourself. Remember that the only tough part about making a homemade pie or tart is the dough. And just like people, the best pies and tarts are imperfect. A little crack here or there, an uneven or a burnt edge tells us you took the time. Rusticity is nice in a pie.

Cheat a little. Use a prepared crust, toss a tart dough together in the food processor, and gradually work your way up to a handmade pie crust. Remember that every honest pie maker has thrown out a few ornery crusts in her day or grown despondent over a delicious filling set atop a tougher-than-nails dough. Still, the good pie maker just keeps on trying. She knows that just like love, good pie making takes time. And the rewards are great!

PRIMAL
PIES

ALL-AMERICAN APPLE PIE

It doesn't get much better than this—a generous double-crusted, browned-on-top, warm and tender, all-American apple pie for wowing the guests.

6 Granny Smith apples, peeled, cored, and cut in large chunks
2 tablespoons lemon juice
$\frac{3}{4}$ cup sugar
1 teaspoon cinnamon
$\frac{1}{4}$ teaspoon allspice
2 tablespoons cornstarch
2 "All-American Pie Crusts" (see page 82)
1 egg white, lightly beaten
sugar for sprinkling

Preheat oven to 425 degrees F.

In a large bowl, combine apples, lemon juice, sugar, cinnamon, allspice, and cornstarch. Toss well.

On a floured board, lightly roll out one piece of dough to 12-inch circle and line a 9-inch pie pan. Fill center with apple mixture. Brush the top edge of the dough with egg white. Roll out the second dough disk. Carefully place over the apples and press the edges together to seal. Crimp the edges. Brush top with egg white and sprinkle with sugar. Cut steam vents in top crust.

Bake 10 minutes on lower rack. Reduce heat to 350 degrees F and bake another 60 to 70 minutes, until the juices are bubbling and top is golden brown. Cool on rack 1 hour.

MAKES 1 PIE

TOTALLY CHERRY PIE

Delicious dark red unsweetened cherries are
available in the supermarket freezer for
year-round pie making.

> 2 (1-pound) bags frozen unsweetened pitted
>   cherries, thawed, *or* 6 cups fresh
> ½ cup sugar
> 1 tablespoon kirsch *or* lemon juice
> 3 tablespoons quick tapioca
> 2 "All-American Pie Crusts" (see page 82)

Preheat oven to 425 degrees F.

In a large bowl, combine cherries, sugar,
kirsch or lemon juice, and tapioca. Stir well
and let sit 15 minutes.

Make the lattice by rolling out one crust
to about 12 inches. With a pizza cutter, pastry wheel, or sharp knife, cut the dough into
½-inch-wide strips. Place on a plate and
chill.

On a floured board, lightly roll out the other crust to a 12-inch circle and line a 9-inch pie pan. Fill center with cherry mixture. Arrange six strips about 1 inch apart across the pie, moistening the edges slightly with water and pressing to seal. Then lay the remaining strips across top to form a checkerboard pattern, sealing the edges.

Bake 30 minutes. Reduce temperature to 350 degrees F and bake 30 minutes longer, until filling is bubbly. Cool on a rack.

MAKES 1 PIE

To Thicken a Pie

The traditional thickeners for an American fruit pie are flour, tapioca, and cornstarch. They can be used interchangeably. Flour cooks up a bit cloudy or creamy, cornstarch turns jellylike, and the best tapioca for pies is tapioca starch or flour. The quick tapioca sold in the supermarket can be used in a pinch. Tapioca starch or flour can be found in health food markets.

MAPLE PEACH PIE WITH PECAN TOPPING

Two Southern favorites are baked to perfection in one bubbling brown pie.

1 "All-American Pie Crust" (see page 82)
6 cups sliced, peeled peaches
$\frac{1}{2}$ cup maple syrup
3 tablespoons cornstarch
$\frac{1}{4}$ teaspoon ground nutmeg
$\frac{1}{2}$ cup all-purpose flour
$\frac{1}{3}$ cup brown sugar
$\frac{3}{4}$ stick butter, cut in small pieces
1 cup roughly chopped pecans

Roll out dough, and line a 9-inch pie plate, crimping the edges. Chill.

In a large bowl, combine peaches, maple syrup, cornstarch, and nutmeg. Let stand 20 minutes. In another small bowl, gently mix together flour, brown sugar, butter, and pecans until crumbly.

Preheat oven to 425 degrees F.

Pour peach mixture into prepared pie crust. Sprinkle nut mixture evenly over top. Bake 15 minutes. Reduce heat to 375 degrees F and bake 40 minutes longer. Cool on rack. Serve warm.

MAKES 1 PIE

RHUBARB PIE

We like our rhubarb straight up, but if you like yours mixed and a little less sour, substitute strawberries—a classic complement—for half the amount of rhubarb.

2 (20-ounce) bags frozen sliced rhubarb, thawed (8 cups)
1½ cups sugar
2 tablespoons lemon juice
3 tablespoons all-purpose flour
2 "All-American Pie Crusts" (see page 82)
2 tablespoons butter, broken in pieces
1 egg beaten with 1 tablespoon water for wash
sugar for sprinkling

Preheat oven to 425 degrees F.

In a large bowl, combine rhubarb, sugar, lemon juice, and flour. Toss well.

On a floured board, lightly roll out one piece of dough, and line a 9-inch pie pan. Fill center with rhubarb mixture. Dot fruit with butter. Brush the top edge of dough with egg white. Roll out the second dough disk. Carefully place over the filling and press the edges together to seal. Crimp the edge. Brush top with egg wash and sprinkle with sugar. Cut steam vents in top crust.

Bake 30 minutes, then reduce to 350 degrees F. Bake an additional 40 minutes until top crust is golden. Cool on rack.

MAKES 1 PIE

SWEET POTATO PIE

This all-American favorite is so easy to make, it's a pity to save it for Thanksgiving.

1 "All-American Pie Crust" (see page 82)
1 large sweet potato, baked and cooled
4 tablespoons butter
2 eggs
2 egg yolks
½ cup brown sugar
¾ cup dark corn syrup
1 tablespoon vanilla
¼ teaspoon allspice

Roll out crust and line a 10-inch tart or pie pan. Chill 30 minutes.

Preheat oven to 375 degrees F. When potato is cool, peel and cut into ½-inch cubes.

Line tart shell with foil, prick with a fork, and fill with weights (see page 70). Bake 10 minutes. Remove from oven and remove weights and foil.

Melt the butter in a small pan over low heat until browned bits are on bottom.

In a large bowl, beat together eggs, yolks, brown sugar, corn syrup, vanilla, and allspice until smooth. Stir in melted butter. Spread the potato cubes in bottom crust. Pour in filling and bake 30 minutes, until tester inserted in center comes out clean. Cool on rack.

MAKES 1 PIE

Confessions of a Pie Crust Impurist
In a pinch, the best substitute for homemade pie or tart crust is the rolled and folded refrigerated type sold in the supermarket in boxes containing two crusts. They are spectacularly easy to work with—simply unfold and press into the pan—and have the taste and flaky texture of a classic American pie crust. Even discriminating guests have been fooled!

CRANBERRY RAISIN CRUMBLE

*When using frozen fruit, be sure to thoroughly
thaw before baking so the fruit doesn't give off
excessive moisture and ruin the crust.*

1 "All-American Pie Crust" (see page 82)
1 (12-ounce) bag frozen cranberries, thawed
   (3 cups)
1 cup raisins
³/₄ cup sugar
1 tablespoon orange liqueur such
   as Grand Marnier
grated zest of 1 small orange
3 tablespoons quick tapioca
double recipe "Crumble Topping"
   (see page 87)

Preheat oven to 350 degrees F. Roll out dough, and line a 9-inch pie plate, crimping the edges. Line with foil, top with weights, and bake 20 minutes. Remove from oven and remove weights and foil.

In a large bowl, combine cranberries, raisins, sugar, orange liqueur, orange zest, and tapioca. Mix well and let sit 15 minutes.

Spoon the cranberry mixture into prebaked pie shell. Cover evenly with crumble and bake 1 hour. Cool on a rack.

MAKES 1 PIE

LEMON MERINGUE PIE

With its majestic white crown, lemon meringue is the queen of American lemon pies. The cake crumbs help the meringue adhere to the top.

  8 eggs
  2¼ cups sugar
  ½ cup plus 1 tablespoon cornstarch
  3 tablespoons all-purpose flour
  2¼ cups water
  2 tablespoons grated lemon zest
  ⅓ cup lemon juice
  3 tablespoons butter
  ¼ teaspoon salt
  1 "All-American Pie Crust" (see page 82), baked and cooled
  ¾ teaspoon cream of tartar
  ¼ cup fine white *or* yellow store-bought cupcakes, crumbled

Separate six eggs. Set aside.

In a medium saucepan, combine 1½ cups sugar with ½ cup of the cornstarch and the flour. Stir in water and cook over medium heat, stirring constantly, until thick. Remove filling from heat.

In a medium bowl, whisk the 6 egg yolks with the remaining 2 whole eggs, then stir several tablespoons of the hot filling mixture into the egg mixture. Pour egg mixture into remaining filling and return pan to heat. Bring to a boil, and cook 3 to 4 minutes, stirring constantly. Remove from heat and stir in lemon zest and juice, butter, and salt. Pour into crust.

Preheat oven to 375 degrees F.

Combine egg whites with cream of tartar and remaining sugar and cornstarch in mixer bowl. Beat until stiff and shiny. Sprinkle cake crumbs evenly over filling. Cover with some meringue, spreading to touch crust all around. Pile remaining meringue on top, swirling with back of spoon. Bake until top begins to brown, about 30 minutes. Refrigerate, uncovered, several hours before serving.

MAKES 1 PIE

KEY LIME PIE

Don't let the difficulty of finding key limes stand between you and this fabulous pie. Ordinary lime juice will do just fine, though key lime juice (from the famous yellow-green Florida limes) is available by mail order from specialty suppliers.

⅔ cup fresh lime juice
1 teaspoon unflavored gelatin
4 egg yolks, lightly beaten
1 (14-ounce) can sweetened condensed milk
1 tablespoon grated lime zest
1 "Graham Cracker Cookie Crumb Crust" (see page 90) *or* "All-American Pie Crust" (see page 82), baked and cooled
2 cups heavy cream, whipped

Pour ¼ cup lime juice into small bowl. Sprinkle gelatin evenly over top and set aside to soften, about 5 minutes.

In top of double boiler, beat yolks with condensed milk. Stir in remaining lime juice and zest. Set over simmering water, and whisk until thickened, about 5 minutes.

Dissolve softened gelatin by setting bowl in a pan of hot water, or microwave on medium about 1 minute. Stir into warm lime mixture, blending well. Remove from heat and pour into prepared crust, smoothing top. Chill until set, 1 hour. Pile whipped cream on top, leaving 1-inch border of filling exposed, or pipe whipped cream as desired. Serve immediately or refrigerate.

MAKES 1 PIE

Georgie Porgie, pudding and pie,
Kissed the girls and made them cry.
When the boys came out to play,
Georgie Porgie ran away.

PUMPKIN PRALINE PIE

Karen has been making this fantastic crunchy-topped pumpkin pie every Thanksgiving since learning about it from a central California restaurateur ten years ago.

1 "All-American Pie Crust" (see page 82)
1 (8-ounce) package cream cheese, softened
¾ cup sugar
2 eggs, lightly beaten
1 (16-ounce) can pumpkin purée
1⅔ cups half-and-half
½ teaspoon salt
1 teaspoon cinnamon
½ teaspoon ground ginger
¼ teaspoon ground cloves
½ stick butter, melted
¾ cup brown sugar
1 cup chopped pecans *or* walnuts

Preheat oven to 425 degrees F.

Roll out dough, and line a 9-inch pie plate, crimping the edges.

In a large mixing bowl, combine cream cheese and sugar. Blend well. Beat in eggs. Add pumpkin, half-and-half, salt, cinnamon, ginger, and cloves. Mix well. Pour into pie crust. Bake 15 minutes. Reduce oven to 350 degrees F and bake 45 minutes longer. Cool on rack.

Combine melted butter, brown sugar, and nuts in small bowl. Spread over cooled pie. Just before serving, place pie under preheated broiler just until topping begins to bubble. Watch carefully to prevent burning.

MAKES 1 PIE

"Promises and pie crust are made to be broken."
    —Jonathan Swift

WHITE CHOCOLATE-GINGER MOUSSE PIE

Sharp ginger and orange liqueur take the edge off the white chocolate's sweetness in this extravagant party pie.

    6 ounces white chocolate, chopped
    ¼ cup half-and-half
    8 ounces cream cheese, softened
    ¾ cup sugar
    3 eggs, separated
    2 tablespoons orange liqueur such as Grand Marnier
    1 cup heavy cream, whipped
    2 tablespoons finely chopped crystallized ginger
    1 "Gingersnap Cookie Crumb Crust" (see page 90), baked and cooled
    white chocolate curls and shredded orange peel for garnish (optional)

In top of double boiler set over simmering water, melt chocolate with half-and-half. Cool until barely warm.

Beat cream cheese and ½ cup sugar, with electric mixer on high speed, until smooth, scraping bowl several times. Add egg yolks and liqueur, and beat to blend. Beat in chocolate mixture just until smooth.

In another bowl, whisk egg whites until soft peaks form. Gradually add remaining sugar, and whisk until firm peaks form. Whisk one-third of whites into chocolate mixture to lighten, then fold in remaining whites. Fold in whipped cream and ginger. Pile mousse into crust, swirling the top. Chill until firm, at least 2 hours. Decorate with chocolate curls and sprinkle with orange peel, if desired.

MAKES 1 PIE

BANANA-RUM CREAM PIE

Banana and silky custard in a nicely made crust is all it takes to make an occasion special.

³/₄ cup sugar
3 tablespoons cornstarch
¹/₄ teaspoon salt
3 cups milk
4 egg yolks, lightly beaten
¹/₂ stick butter, cut in pieces
2 tablespoons rum *or* 1¹/₂ teaspoons vanilla
3 bananas, peeled and sliced
1 "Graham Cracker Cookie Crumb Crust"
  (see page 90) *or* "All-American Pie Crust"
  (see page 82), baked and cooled
1¹/₂ cups heavy cream, whipped

In saucepan, combine sugar, cornstarch, and salt. Gradually whisk in milk and yolks. Set over medium heat and bring to a boil, stirring constantly. Reduce heat and simmer, stirring, about 3 minutes, or until very thick. Remove from heat and stir in butter and rum. Cover with plastic wrap and set aside to cool.

Meanwhile, arrange slices of two bananas in a circular pattern over bottom and sides of crust. Pour in filling, smoothing the top. Chill at least 2 hours. Just before serving, top pie with whipped cream. Arrange remaining banana slices around edges.

MAKES 1 PIE

COCONUT CREAM PIE

We are suckers for coconut baked into just about anything, but this pie takes the cake. Unsweetened coconut is available at health and organic food markets.

2 cups shredded unsweetened coconut, toasted
1 recipe "Pastry Cream Supreme" (see page 92)
1 "All-American Pie Crust" (see page 82),
    baked and cooled
1 cup heavy cream, cold
½ cup confectioners' sugar

Fold 1½ cups of coconut into warm pastry cream. Pour into cooled pie shell and smooth top. Chill about 2 hours.

Whip the heavy cream until soft peaks form. Add sugar, and beat until thick. Spread over coconut cream. Sprinkle top with remaining toasted coconut. Serve or store in the refrigerator.

MAKES 1 PIE

CLASSIC PECAN PIE

Who can resist a sticky, gooey, just-sweet-enough slice of pecan pie? Not us, never.

1 "All-American Pie Crust" (see page 82)
3 eggs plus 1 yolk, beaten
¾ cup brown sugar
1 cup dark corn syrup
¼ teaspoon salt
1 tablespoon rum *or* vanilla
½ stick butter, melted
2 cups pecan halves

Preheat oven to 350 degrees F. Roll out dough, and line a 9-inch pie pan, crimping the edges.

In a large bowl, stir together eggs, sugar, corn syrup, salt, and rum or vanilla. Stir in butter and then pecans. Pour into pie shell. Bake about 40 to 50 minutes, until just set. Cool on a rack.

MAKES 1 PIE

LEMON CHESS PIE

Chess pie, with its concentration of eggs and butter, is a Southern baking tradition. Play with the flavor by replacing lemon with vanilla extract or another citrus, such as lime or orange.

1 "All-American Pie Crust" (see page 82)
1¾ cups sugar
3 tablespoons all-purpose flour
grated zest and juice of 3 lemons
6 eggs, lightly beaten
1 stick butter, melted

Preheat oven to 325 degrees F.

Roll out dough, and line a 9-inch pie plate, crimping the edges.

In a large bowl, mix sugar, flour, and lemon zest. Stir in lemon juice, then beat in eggs. Add butter, and beat well. Pour into dough-lined pan. Bake 45 minutes, or until puffy and golden but wobbly in center. Cool on rack. Refrigerate if not serving immediately. Return to room temperature before serving.

MAKES 1 PIE

The Pie-Making Equipment List

- Glass pie plates, *the inexpensive kind sold in hardware stores and supermarkets, are the best since you can see the bottom and sides of the crust to check for browning.*
- *For tarts, we love French* tart pans with removable bottoms. *Once the tart has cooled, just remove the sides and place the bottom sheet on your favorite platter for an elegant display. Black tins cook hotter and faster, so adjust times accordingly. These recipes were tested in silvery metal tins.*
- Tinfoil pie pans, *sold in bulk at the supermarket, are handy for baking a pie you plan to bring to a pot luck or bake sale. No fear of equipment loss.*
- *The best* rolling pin *is whatever the baker feels most comfortable with. Professionals, as a rule,*

prefer heavy pins with rolling handles since they demand the least amount of body weight and wrist work to get the job done. Avoid nicking the pin by rolling it over tops of metal tart tins to trim crusts, and don't assiduously scrub clean with soap and water. Lightly wash, as you would a cast-iron pan, to keep the wood seasoned for less sticking.

- Pastry blenders, *the wooden-handled metal-pronged half-moons, are good for beginning to blend cold fat and flour for a handmade pie crust. Switch to your fingers to finish blending and learn the proper consistency.*

- Pastry scrapers *for lifting a sticky dough from the board and a* pastry brush *reserved especially for brushing away excess flour (one that is not oily and stiff from old marinades and glazes) are handy to have around, as is a* pizza cutter *for cutting a lattice. Of utmost importance is the* pie server, *an offset triangular spatula, for lifting those succulent slices from their cozy pie pans onto eagerly awaiting plates.*

UPTOWN TARTS

VERY BERRY TART

*Our shiny, red berry tart is not only beautiful,
it is virtuous as well. The filling isn't cream,
but healthful yogurt. Make sure all the fruit is
washed and thoroughly dried for best results.*

1 quart plain yogurt
1 cup sugar
½ teaspoon vanilla
1 "Shortbread Tart Crust" (see page 84) *or*
    "Graham *or* Shortbread Cookie Crumb
    Crust" (see page 90), baked and cooled
3½ cups strawberries, hulled and halved
1 cup raspberries
1 cup blueberries
1 tablespoon cornstarch
1 teaspoon lemon juice

A day in advance, place yogurt in colander lined with cheesecloth. Set colander in a bowl, and cover with plastic wrap. Refrigerate at least 12 hours. Transfer drained yogurt to mixing bowl. Whisk in ½ cup sugar and vanilla.

Spread yogurt evenly over prepared crust. Starting at outside edge, arrange about 2 cups strawberries, cut-sides up, in concentric circles, leaving an empty space in the center. Mix raspberries and blueberries, and pile in the center, partially covering the strawberries.

Purée remaining strawberries in blender. Transfer to saucepan and whisk in remaining sugar and cornstarch. Bring to a boil over medium heat. Boil, whisking frequently, until opaque, about 1 minute. Remove from heat, and stir in lemon juice. Cool to lukewarm, then spoon over tart, covering berries completely. Refrigerate at least 2 hours before serving.

MAKES 1 TART

CHOCOLATE SILK TART

If you like your chocolate simple, elegant, and straight-on, you will adore this sophisticated French tart.

1 "Shortbread Tart Crust" (see page 84)
1 cup half-and-half
8 ounces bittersweet chocolate, finely chopped
1 egg, beaten
cocoa powder *or* confectioners' sugar, for garnish (optional)

Roll out dough, and line 9-inch tart pan. Chill 30 minutes. Preheat oven to 375 degrees F.

Line the crust with aluminum foil, and prick a few times with a fork. Line with weights. Bake 25 minutes, until edges tan. Remove from oven, remove weights and foil, and set aside to cool, leaving oven on.

Bring half-and-half to a simmer in a heavy pot over moderate heat. Remove from heat, add chocolate, and stir until melted and smooth. Cool to room temperature and stir in egg.

Pour into cooled tart shell, and bake an additional 15 minutes, until set but slightly wobbly in center. Cool on rack, and then dust, if desired, with cocoa or sugar. Serve warm or at room temperature.

MAKES 1 TART

The Queen of Hearts,
She made some tarts,
All on a summer's day.
The Knave of Hearts,
He stole those tarts,
And took them clean away.

PEAR ALMOND TART

Some other fruits to serve baked in almond cream are plums and peaches, halved and pitted.

1 "Shortbread Tart Crust" (see page 84)
4 ripe pears
1 recipe "Almond Cream" (see page 94)
confectioners' sugar for dusting

On a lightly floured board, roll out dough, and line a 10-inch tart pan. Chill 15 minutes.

Preheat oven to 350 degrees F. Peel pears, cut in half lengthwise, and core. Place cut-side down on board, and thinly slice across width.

Line the crust with aluminum foil and prick a few times with a fork. Fill with weights and bake 20 minutes. Remove from oven and remove weights and foil. Spread almond cream over bottom. Lift each pear half with a small spatula or butter knife and fan the slices. Arrange over cream, with thin ends pointing to center. Bake until edges are golden and almond cream is set, about 50 minutes. Cool on a rack. Dust with confectioners' sugar and serve.

MAKES 1 TART

LEMON TART

This is the elegant tarte au citron *of French pastry shop fame. Serve it cold on a hot summer's day for maximum audience response.*

1 "Simple Tart Crust" (see page 86)
6 tablespoons butter, softened
$^2/_3$ cup sugar
3 eggs
$^1/_4$ cup heavy cream
grated zest and juice of 3 lemons

Preheat oven to 425 degrees F.

On a lightly floured board, roll out dough, and line a 10-inch tart pan. Chill 15 minutes.

Line the crust with aluminum foil, and prick a few times with a fork. Fill with weights and bake 15 minutes. Remove from oven and remove weights and foil. Reduce oven to 325 degrees F.

In a large bowl, beat together the butter and sugar with mixer until light. Beat in the eggs and cream. Then beat in the lemon zest and juice. (Do not worry about curdling.) Pour into prebaked shell. Bake about 1 hour, until crust is golden and top begins to brown. Cool on a rack, then chill.

MAKES 1 TART

MOCHA TART

If you have a large (12-inch) pan, use it for this rich, caffeine-intensive mousse tart. If using a smaller pan, leftover mousse can be kept up to 2 days in the refrigerator for clandestine snacking.

1½ cups heavy cream, cold
1 tablespoon coffee liqueur such as Kahlua
1 teaspoon very finely ground espresso
    beans
8 ounces bittersweet chocolate, chopped
4 egg whites
6 tablespoons sugar
1 "Shortbread *or* Chocolate Wafer Cookie
    Crumb Crust" (see page 90), baked and
    cooled
chocolate-dipped espresso beans (optional)
    for garnish

Whip 1 cup of the heavy cream until thickened. Add coffee liqueur and continue beating until stiff peaks form. Chill.

In a small pot, combine the remaining cream and espresso beans. Bring to a simmer, add the chocolate, and remove from heat. Stir with a spoon until melted and smooth. Set aside to cool.

In a clean bowl, whisk the egg whites until foamy. Add sugar and continue whisking until stiff peaks form. Fold in melted chocolate in two parts. Then fold in whipped cream until smooth. Fill the tart shell, smoothing the top. Chill for at least 2 hours before serving. Decorate the top with espresso beans if desired.

MAKES 1 TART

Simple Simon met a pieman,
Going to the fair.
Says Simple Simon to the pieman,
"Let me taste your ware."

ROASTED PEACHES AND RICOTTA TART

Make the crust the night before for a special breakfast or brunch treat.

1 "Simple Tart Crust" (see page 86), baked and cooled
"Apricot Glaze" (see page 95)
3 large peaches, pitted and cut in 8 wedges
$\frac{1}{4}$ cup sugar
2 tablespoons butter
$2\frac{1}{2}$ cups ricotta cheese
3 tablespoons honey

Preheat oven to 425 degrees F. Brush the cooled crust with apricot glaze.

In a ceramic or glass baking dish, toss peaches with sugar. Dot with butter and bake, uncovered, 30 minutes. Cool slightly in juices.

In a mixing bowl, stir together ricotta and honey. Spoon into tart shell, smoothing the top. With slotted spoon, leaving excess juices in the pan, ladle peach slices on top and serve immediately. This delicate tart is best eaten within the hour, since moisture will seep through to the crust.

MAKES 1 TART

STRAWBERRY RHUBARB TART

When strawberries and rhubarb are cooked together, the rhubarb takes on the color of the berries and seems to disappear.

3 cups ¹/₂-inch rhubarb slices, fresh *or* frozen, thawed
²/₃ cup sugar
1¹/₂ teaspoons grated orange zest
¹/₄ teaspoon ground ginger
3 cups hulled and halved strawberries
1 "Simple Tart Crust" (see page 86), baked and cooled
1 cup heavy cream
¹/₄ cup confectioners' sugar

In a saucepan, combine rhubarb and sugar, and let stand 15 minutes or until juices are released. Stir in 1 teaspoon orange zest and half the ginger. Toss well. Place over medium heat, cover, and cook until rhubarb is tender, about 10 minutes. Remove from heat and stir in berries. Transfer to bowl, cover, and chill several hours. Pour fruit mixture into crust. Refrigerate until serving time.

In a large bowl, whisk cream and confectioners' sugar until medium thick. Add remaining orange zest and ginger, and whisk until thick. Pass at the table to spoon over tart wedges.

MAKES 1 TART

Sing a song of sixpence,
A pocket full of rye;
Four-and-twenty blackbirds,
Baked in a pie.

BLUEBERRY NECTARINE TART

This is a decorative and delicious choice for late-summer entertaining.

1 " Shortbread Tart Crust" (see page 84) *or*
  "Simple Tart Crust" (see page 86)
4 cups blueberries, fresh *or* frozen, thawed
1 cup sugar
2 tablespoons all-purpose flour
1 teaspoon cinnamon
2 tablespoons lemon juice
4 nectarines, sliced

Preheat oven to 425 degrees F.

On a lightly floured board, roll out dough, and line a 10-inch tart pan.

In a large bowl, combine blueberries with $3/4$ cup sugar, flour, cinnamon, and lemon juice. Toss well. Set aside $3/4$ cup of berry mixture. Spoon remaining berry mixture over crust. Arrange nectarine slices over berries in concentric circles, leaving $1 1/2$ inches bare on edges. Sprinkle evenly with remaining sugar. Spoon reserved berry mixture into center.

Bake 30 minutes. Reduce oven temperature to 350 degrees F and bake 45 minutes longer, until fruit is bubbly. Cool on rack.

MAKES 1 TART

ITALIAN PLUM-ALMOND TART

Small, purple prune plums have a short season in California—just August and September. Feel free to use any other small plum that is in the market.

1 "Simple Tart Crust" (see page 86)
¾ cup sugar
1 cup all-purpose flour
4 teaspoons cinnamon
20 Italian prune plums, halved and pitted
1 stick butter
1 cup toasted whole almonds
½ cup brown sugar
¼ teaspoon salt

Preheat oven to 425 degrees F.

On a lightly floured board, roll out dough, and line a 10-inch tart pan.

Combine sugar, $\frac{1}{3}$ cup flour, and cinnamon in bowl. Toss well. Sprinkle half of mixture over bottom of crust. Starting from outside edge, arrange plum halves, overlapping, cut-side up, in a circular pattern. Sprinkle remaining sugar mixture over plums. Dot with 2 tablespoons butter. Bake 10 minutes. Remove tart from oven and reduce temperature to 350 degrees F.

Meanwhile, chop almonds in food processor until coarsely ground. Add remaining flour, brown sugar, salt, and remaining butter, cut in pieces. Process just to blend, about 10 seconds.

Sprinkle almond topping over plums, and return to oven. Bake 30 minutes longer, until plums are bubbly and topping is golden.

MAKES 1 TART

FIG TART

A simple tart such as this highlights the taste of fresh fruit. Leave the skins on to add color and texture.

1 "Simple Tart Crust" (see page 86)
¼ cup whole almonds
¼ cup sugar
2 tablespoons all-purpose flour
1½ pounds ripe figs, trimmed and quartered
1 tablespoon butter
additional sugar for sprinkling (optional)

Preheat oven to 425 degrees F.

Roll out tart dough, and line a 10-inch tart pan. Chill.

Combine the almonds, sugar, and flour in a food processor and finely grind. Sprinkle over lined tart shell, and top with a single layer of fig wedges. Dot with butter, and sprinkle with sugar if desired. Bake 30 minutes. Reduce heat to 375 degrees F and bake 20 to 30 minutes longer until crust is golden and fruit bubbly. Cool on rack.

MAKES 1 TART

APRICOT TART

*Whatever happened to great apricots? If you
happen to know someone with a backyard tree,
promise them a tart in exchange for a few bags
of the real ripe thing.*

1 "Shortbread Tart Crust" (see page 84)
½ cup heavy cream
1 egg
⅓ cup sugar
1 tablespoon all-purpose flour
1 teaspoon vanilla
1 pound fresh apricots, pitted and halved

On a lightly floured board, roll out dough and line a 10-inch tart pan. Chill 15 minutes.

Preheat oven to 375 degrees F.

Line the crust with aluminum foil, and prick a few times with a fork. Fill with weights, and bake 10 minutes. Remove from oven and remove weights and foil. Reduce oven to 325 degrees F.

In a bowl, whisk together cream and egg. Whisk in sugar, flour, and vanilla. Pour into partially baked tart shell, top with apricots cut-side up, and bake 30 to 40 minutes, until set. Cool on rack.

MAKES 1 TART

APPLE BLUEBERRY CRUMBLE TART

A warm slice of this tender tart, topped with a dollop of plain yogurt, would be a heavenly breakfast.

1 "Shortbread Tart Crust" (see page 84)
4 small Golden Delicious apples, peeled, cored, and sliced
1 cup blueberries
2 tablespoons lemon juice
$\frac{1}{4}$ cup sugar
$\frac{1}{4}$ teaspoon cinnamon
1 recipe "Crumble Topping" (see page 87)

Preheat oven to 375 degrees F. Roll out the dough, and line a 9-inch tart pan. Line the crust with aluminum foil, and prick a few times with a fork. Fill with weights and bake 15 minutes. Remove from oven and remove weights and foil.

Meanwhile, toss together the apples, blueberries, lemon juice, sugar, and cinnamon in a bowl.

Spoon apple mixture into partially baked tart shell, leaving liquid in bowl. Sprinkle crumble topping evenly over fruit, and bake 45 to 55 minutes, until crust is golden brown. Serve warm or at room temperature.

MAKES 1 TART

How to Roll a Crust

To make a good pie crust takes cool fingers and a warm heart, or so the saying goes. First, remove chilled dough and let rest on a counter 15 to 30 minutes to warm slightly. You can quickly warm a too-cold disk of dough by pressing it in the palms of your hands or hitting it a few times with a rolling pin. Dough that is too warm or sticky should be placed back in the refrigerator for a few minutes to harden slightly. Novices may be best off to roll dough between two sheets of plastic wrap to avoid sticking altogether. The plastic just peels off.

Lightly dust the board and top of dough with flour and start rolling from the center out, lifting and making quarter-turns with the dough, and flipping over, to prevent sticking. Lower the pin, and roll gently—bashing with the pin is cruel and toughens the dough. Tears in the dough can be repaired by rolling the broken edges toward each other and then sprinkling with a little flour, if necessary. To lift the dough, fold in half, brushing off excess flour, and lower into the pan. Unfold and press into pan, brushing off excess flour again. Torn dough can be patched in the pan with extra dough scraps. Since, by now, the dough is probably warm, chill about 30 minutes before baking.

PIES FOR ONE

BLACKBERRY CHOCOLATE TART

Something this good and rich is lovely when presented as an individual gem—though the recipe can be made in a larger pan.

8 ounces bittersweet chocolate, chopped
1 cup heavy cream
1 "Shortbread Tart Crust" (see page 84), baked and cooled in 4 mini-tins
2 pints blackberries, washed and dried

Place half the chocolate in a medium bowl. Bring the cream to a boil. Pour, all at once, over the chocolate, and whisk by hand until smooth. Chill until very cold.

Before serving, melt the remaining chocolate in a microwave at high power for 1 minute. Stir until smooth, and then brush over bottom of baked tart shells. Chill 15 minutes to set.

Remove the chilled chocolate cream and, with an electric mixer, whisk about 1 minute at medium speed until thick enough to spread. Spoon into tart shells and evenly spread. Arrange berries on top, and chill or serve.

MAKES 4 MINI-TARTS

HOT PEAR TARTS

Serve these rich dessert pastries straight out of the oven as a showstopper at the end of an elegant feast.

6 tablespoons butter
6 ripe pears, peeled, cored, and thinly sliced
⅓ cup sugar
2 tablespoons pear brandy
1 pound frozen puff pastry, thawed
confectioners' sugar for dusting

Preheat oven to 400 degrees F.

In a large saucepan, melt butter over medium-high heat. Add the pears and sugar, and cook, stirring frequently, until golden, about 10 minutes.

Place half the pears in a blender or food processor. Add brandy and purée. Chill, along with remaining slices in a separate container, 30 minutes.

Roll out pastry to ¼-inch thickness. With a floured cutter or a glass, cut pastry into six 4-inch circles, and place on uncoated baking sheets. Spread each pastry circle with pear purée, leaving ½ inch bare along the edge. Top each with fanned pear slices. Bake 35 to 40 minutes, until pastry is puffed and brown. Dust with confectioners' sugar and serve hot.

MAKES 6 TARTS

How to Prebake a Crust

Shells for cold mousse or custard pies are fully baked and cooled, and some fruit pies with a creamy filling are partially baked, to prevent soggy bottom crusts. Bakers call baking an empty tart or pie shell baking blind.

To partially bake a tart shell, line with foil and prick all over with a fork. Chill 30 minutes. Fill with weights, rice, or beans, and bake in the lower third of a 325-degree F oven until crust is just set, about 10 to 15 minutes. If the foil sticks, return to oven, and bake a bit longer. Remove foil and save weights to use again.

To fully bake a tart shell, line as above with foil and weights and bake 15 minutes. Then remove weights and bake 20 to 25 minutes longer, until golden.

To fully bake an All-American pie crust, prick all over with a fork, and bake, unlined, in a 450-degree F oven about 15 minutes, until lightly browned.

MEALS-IN-A-PIE

CORN AND CHILE PIE

The overlapping edges of tortilla crust form a scalloped edge in this lovely vegetarian pie.

vegetable oil
6 taco-size corn tortillas
1 onion, diced
1 to 2 jalapeño chiles, stemmed, seeded, and chopped *or* 1 (7-ounce) can diced green chiles
1½ cups corn kernels, fresh *or* frozen
2 cups shredded Monterey Jack cheese
4 eggs, beaten
1 cup milk
½ teaspoon salt
¼ teaspoon pepper

Preheat oven to 350 degrees F.

Coat a small pan with oil, and place over low heat. Briefly fry tortillas just to soften. Arrange tortillas in 9- or 10-inch pie plate, overlapping to cover bottom and overhang the edges about 1½ inches.

Heat 2 tablespoons of oil in a large skillet over medium-high heat. Sauté onion until soft. Stir in chiles and corn kernels, and sauté about 1 minute longer. Transfer mixture to lined pie plate. Sprinkle cheese over the top.

In a bowl, beat together eggs, milk, salt, and pepper. Pour over filling. Bake about 45 minutes, or until almost set in center. Cool 10 minutes before serving.

SERVES 8

SWISS CHARD-TOMATO PIE

Chard is one of our favorite leafy greens. Because they are tough, the stems must be boiled before they are cooked with the leaves. You can save time by just trimming and discarding the stems if necessary.

1 "All-American Pie Crust" (see page 82)
1 large bunch green Swiss chard
2 tablespoons olive oil
1 onion, diced
2 garlic cloves, minced
¼ cup cooked crumbled bacon (optional)
1 teaspoon grated lemon zest
salt and pepper to taste
1½ cups shredded fontina cheese
2 eggs
¾ cup milk
¾ pound tomatoes, sliced
½ cup Italian bread crumbs
¼ cup grated Parmesan cheese

On a lightly floured board, roll out dough, and line a 9-inch pie pan. Chill.

Rinse chard well and trim about 1 inch off stems. Cut remaining stems from leaves, and chop. Bring 2 cups water to boil in a saucepan. Add chard stems, and return to boil. Reduce heat, cover, and simmer 10 minutes. Roughly chop chard leaves.

Meanwhile, heat oil in a large skillet over medium-high heat. Sauté onion and garlic until soft, about 5 minutes. Add Swiss chard leaves, reduce heat, cover, and simmer until wilted, about 5 minutes. Drain stems, and add to leaves. Raise heat to medium-high, and cook, uncovered, turning several times until pan is nearly dry. Transfer to strainer and press out any excess moisture. Transfer chard to bowl. Stir in bacon, if desired, lemon zest, salt, and pepper.

Preheat oven to 350 degrees F.

Spread half of fontina cheese evenly over bottom crust. Arrange chard mixture over cheese. Spread remaining fontina on top. Beat eggs with milk, and pour over filling. Arrange tomato slices in concentric circles on top. Combine bread crumbs and Parmesan in bowl, and sprinkle evenly over tomatoes. Bake 45 minutes, or until set. Cool slightly before serving.

SERVES 6 TO 8

A Short History of the Pie

Savory pies have been around since the time of the ancient Greeks. But in the long history of pies, a pastry crust filled with sweetened fruit is a fairly recent phenomenon—beginning in the early sixteenth century in France and England. Prior to that, a pie was a big, sturdy vessel for carrying and preserving all kinds of meats (occasionally mixed with sweets, such as mincemeat), as well as four-and-twenty blackbirds, as has been documented in the famous nursery rhyme.

Recipes for fruit pies, most notably apple, were brought to the New World by the Pilgrims. From Plymouth colony, pie spread like wildfire as an all-purpose food suitable for serving at breakfast, lunch, dinner, and snack time. The expressions "American as apple pie" and "easy as pie" were coined because, in fact, pie was so commonplace in the American diet that the typical home cook made several pies a day. And if you make that many pies, it does get easy.

CHICKEN POTPIE WITH BEER-BATTER CRUST

Chicken potpie is another one of those dishes, like apple pie, that conjures images of home and hearth.

1½ sticks butter
2 onions, roughly chopped
2 cups peeled baby carrots, cut in half
2 celery stalks, sliced
4 cups cooked chicken meat, in chunks
2 tablespoons chopped parsley
1 teaspoon poultry seasoning
2 cups plus 3 tablespoons all-purpose flour
1¾ cups chicken broth
1 cup beer
1 cup frozen peas, thawed
salt and pepper
2 teaspoons baking powder

In a large skillet, melt 2 tablespoons of butter over medium-high heat. Add onions, and cook, stirring occasionally, until soft. Add carrots and celery, and cook about 5 minutes longer, or until tender. Stir in chicken, parsley, and poultry seasoning. Remove from heat.

In a saucepan, melt 4 tablespoons of butter over medium-high heat. Sprinkle in 3 tablespoons flour, stirring constantly, until smooth. Gradually add chicken broth and $\frac{1}{2}$ cup beer, stirring frequently until mixture is thick, about 5 minutes. Stir in peas and chicken mixture. Season to taste with salt and pepper. Transfer to a shallow 2-quart casserole.

Preheat oven to 425 degrees F.

In a bowl, sift remaining flour with baking powder and 1 teaspoon salt. Cut in 4 tablespoons butter until crumbly. Pour in remaining $\frac{1}{2}$ cup beer, tossing mixture with a fork until a dough begins to form. Turn out onto floured surface and briefly knead. Roll dough out to fit casserole. Carefully transfer to top of chicken mixture. (It is not necessary to tuck in edges.) If desired, score dough with sharp knife to make a diamond design. Melt remaining 2 tablespoons butter, and brush on crust. Bake 15 minutes, or until top is puffy and golden.

SERVES 8

"...It seems to me that mere chemistry can explain what makes a cake, while pie demands metaphysics. The opposition between a pie's inside and out, the dialectic, if you will, between crust and filling, can't but set minds wondering."

—Judith Moore, Never Eat Your Heart Out

INCREDIBLE CRUSTS, PLUMP FILLINGS, AND CRYSTAL GLAZES

ALL-AMERICAN PIE CRUST

The best technique for learning to make a home-made crust is to watch an experienced baker—several times—before trying. Then get ready to toss out lots of disasters until your fingertips learn their lesson. The overriding principle to keep in mind is not to overwork the dough—a light touch and a minimum of worry is best.

2½ cups all-purpose flour
2 teaspoons sugar
½ teaspoon salt
1 stick butter, cold, cut in ½-inch slices
½ cup shortening, cold, in tablespoon-size
    pieces
6 tablespoons cold water

In a large mixing bowl, combine flour, sugar, and salt. Add butter and shortening. Combine by pinching with fingertips or pastry blender until fat is evenly distributed and broken into hazelnut-size pieces. (The mixture should hold together when pressed.) Add water all at once, and stir a few times with a wooden spoon. Turn out onto plastic wrap, and loosely wrap. Gently knead into a ball and then divide in half. Covering each with plastic, press into 5-inch disks, and wrap well. Chill 1 hour to 3 days or freeze for later use.

MAKES TWO 9-INCH PIE CRUSTS

"Perfect American pie crust must be seven things at once—flaky, airy, light, tender, crisp, well browned, and good tasting."

> —*Jeffrey Steingarten,* The Man Who Ate Everything

SHORTBREAD TART CRUST

This sweet, crumbly dough is a bit tricky to work with. Be sure to chill before rolling.

1¼ cups pastry flour
½ cup confectioners' sugar
pinch of salt
6 tablespoons butter, cold, cut in pieces
1 egg yolk beaten with ½ teaspoon vanilla

In a food processor fitted with the metal blade, combine flour, sugar, and salt. Pulse to mix. Add butter, and pulse to break into small pieces. Add yolk mixture. Pulse until mixture is crumbly and holds together when pressed. Transfer to plastic sheet, press into a disk, wrap, and chill 1 hour to 2 days.

MAKES ONE 9- OR 10-INCH TART CRUST

VARIATION:
To make a food processor crust by hand, combine the dry ingredients in a mixing bowl. Blend in the cold butter or shortening until a crumbly mixture forms, stir in the egg or liquid, and gently knead to form a disk.

SIMPLE TART CRUST

Here is an easy, almost foolproof all-purpose crust.

- 1 cup all-purpose flour
- 1 teaspoon sugar
- pinch of salt
- 7 tablespoons cold butter, cut in slices
- 2 tablespoons cold water

In a food processor with the metal blade, combine flour, sugar, and salt. Pulse to combine. Add butter, and pulse briefly just until mixture resembles coarse meal. Add the water and pulse a few times, until pastry holds together when pressed. Transfer to work surface, press into a disk, and wrap in plastic. Chill 30 minutes to 2 days.

MAKES ONE 9-INCH TART CRUST

CRUMBLE TOPPING

The key to a pebbly crumble topping is not to overwork the flour and butter. Crumble can be made in advance and kept in the refrigerator for emergency crisps, muffins, tarts, and pies.

$\frac{1}{3}$ cup brown sugar
$\frac{1}{2}$ stick butter, softened
$\frac{1}{4}$ teaspoon cinnamon
pinch of nutmeg and salt
$\frac{3}{4}$ cup all-purpose flour

Cream together sugar, butter, cinnamon, nutmeg, and salt until fluffy. Gently mix in flour just until crumbly.

MAKES 1 CUP

FOOD PROCESSOR PÂTÉ SUCRÉ

The first tart dough we ever learned is virtually foolproof, especially if you roll it out between sheets of plastic wrap. Substitute in any recipe calling for "Simple" or "Shortbread" crust, and omit sugar for the classic quiche dough—pâté brisé.

1 cup all-purpose flour
2 tablespoons sugar
pinch of salt
1 stick cold butter, cut into 8 pieces
1 egg yolk
1½ tablespoons cold water
½ teaspoon vanilla

Combine the flour, sugar, and salt in a food processor fitted with the metal blade. Process briefly. Add pieces of butter, and pulse until large chunks of butter are visible.

In a small bowl, with a fork, beat together egg yolk, water, and vanilla. With the food processor running, pour egg mixture through the feed tube, and process until a dough ball forms on the blade. Press into a disk, cover with plastic, and chill 30 minutes or longer.

MAKES ONE 10-INCH TART CRUST

COOKIE CRUMB CRUSTS

Cookie crusts are the easiest for beginners. There is no dough to roll—just use your fingers to press the mixture into the pan. Crush the cookies with a food processor or rolling pin.

2 cups fine cookie crumbs such as graham
    cracker, gingersnap, shortbread, *or*
    chocolate wafer
melted butter
confectioners' sugar

Preheat oven to 325 degrees F.

Combine crumbs and butter in a bowl, using 1 stick for graham and gingersnap crusts, ³/₄ stick for shortbread or chocolate wafer crusts. Mix until smooth, adding sugar to taste. Press evenly onto bottom and sides of 9-inch pie plate. Top with empty 8-inch pie plate, and press down to pack. Shape edge to make even. Bake 5 minutes. Cool before filling.

MAKES ONE 9-INCH CRUST

VARIATION:
Replace ³/₄ cup crumbs with ³/₄ cup finely chopped nuts, such as pecans with gingersnaps; hazelnuts or walnuts with shortbreads; or almonds or pecans with chocolate wafers.

PASTRY CREAM SUPREME

This easy stovetop custard can be made in advance and kept in the refrigerator for about a week. Fold in bananas or coconut to fill a baked tart shell or make a pastry cream-and-fruit tart with sweet, juicy apricots or peaches.

1/2 cup sugar
2 tablespoons all-purpose flour
2 tablespoons cornstarch
2 eggs
3 cups milk
1 1/2 teaspoons vanilla

Mix together the sugar, flour, cornstarch, and eggs in a bowl with a fork.

Pour the milk into a large, heavy saucepan. Bring to a boil. Gradually ladle half the hot milk into egg mixture, whisking constantly. Then pour milk-and-egg mixture back into saucepan. Cook, whisking constantly, over medium heat until bubbly and thick, about 5 minutes. Remove from heat, add vanilla, and continue whisking about 5 minutes to cool down. Cool slightly, pour into a bowl, cover with plastic (not touching the cream's surface), and store in the refrigerator.

To bake pastry cream topped with fruit, first prebake empty shell 10 minutes at 325 degrees F. Fill with custard layer (about half the recipe) and bake an additional 10 minutes, until set but not browned. Top with fruit and bake until fruit is tender, 20 to 30 minutes.

MAKES ENOUGH FOR 2 PIES

ALMOND CREAM

This French-style cream filling, also called frangipane, *is a cinch to make. It keeps in the refrigerator for about a week and is delicious spread on sliced brioche and toasted.*

$\frac{1}{2}$ cup sugar
$\frac{1}{2}$ cup blanched almonds
6 tablespoons butter, softened
1 egg
1 egg yolk
1 tablespoon rum

Combine the sugar and almonds in a food processor fitted with the metal blade. Finely grind. Add the butter, 1 tablespoon at a time, and process between additions until smooth. Beat together the egg, yolk, and rum in a small bowl. Add to food processor, and process until smooth. Store in the refrigerator as long as 1 week.

MAKES 2 CUPS, ENOUGH FOR ONE 10-INCH TART

APRICOT GLAZE

Dab glaze on lightly with a brush to give fruit added sheen after baking. Use to glaze stone fruit like peaches, plums, and apricots. It's also great with apples and pears.

- ½ cup apricot preserves, poor quality
- ¼ cup sugar
- ¼ cup water

Combine all the ingredients in a small pan. Bring to a boil, reduce to a simmer, and cook, stirring and skimming off foam, until glossy, about 10 minutes. Strain and cool before using. Warm over low heat if too thick to spread. Brush on glaze.

MAKES ENOUGH FOR 2 TARTS

VARIATION:
Use the same method with red currant jelly for glazing berry tarts.

CONVERSIONS

LIQUID
1 Tbsp = 15 ml
½ cup = 4 fl oz = 125 ml
1 cup = 8 fl oz = 250 ml

DRY
¼ cup = 4 Tbsp = 2 oz = 60 g
1 cup = ½ pound = 8 oz = 250 g

FLOUR
½ cup = 60 g
1 cup = 4 oz = 125 g

TEMPERATURE
400° F = 200° C = gas mark 6
375° F = 190° C = gas mark 5
350° F = 175° C = gas mark 4

MISCELLANEOUS
2 Tbsp butter = 1 oz = 30 g
1 inch = 2.5 cm
all-purpose flour = plain flour
baking soda = bicarbonate of soda
brown sugar = demerara sugar
heavy cream = double cream
sugar = caster sugar
kirsch = cherry brandy